I0606063
ANGIE THOMAS
HIP-HOP AUTHOR AND
VOICE OF CHANGE

Desert Rose
CAFE
OPEN
24-7

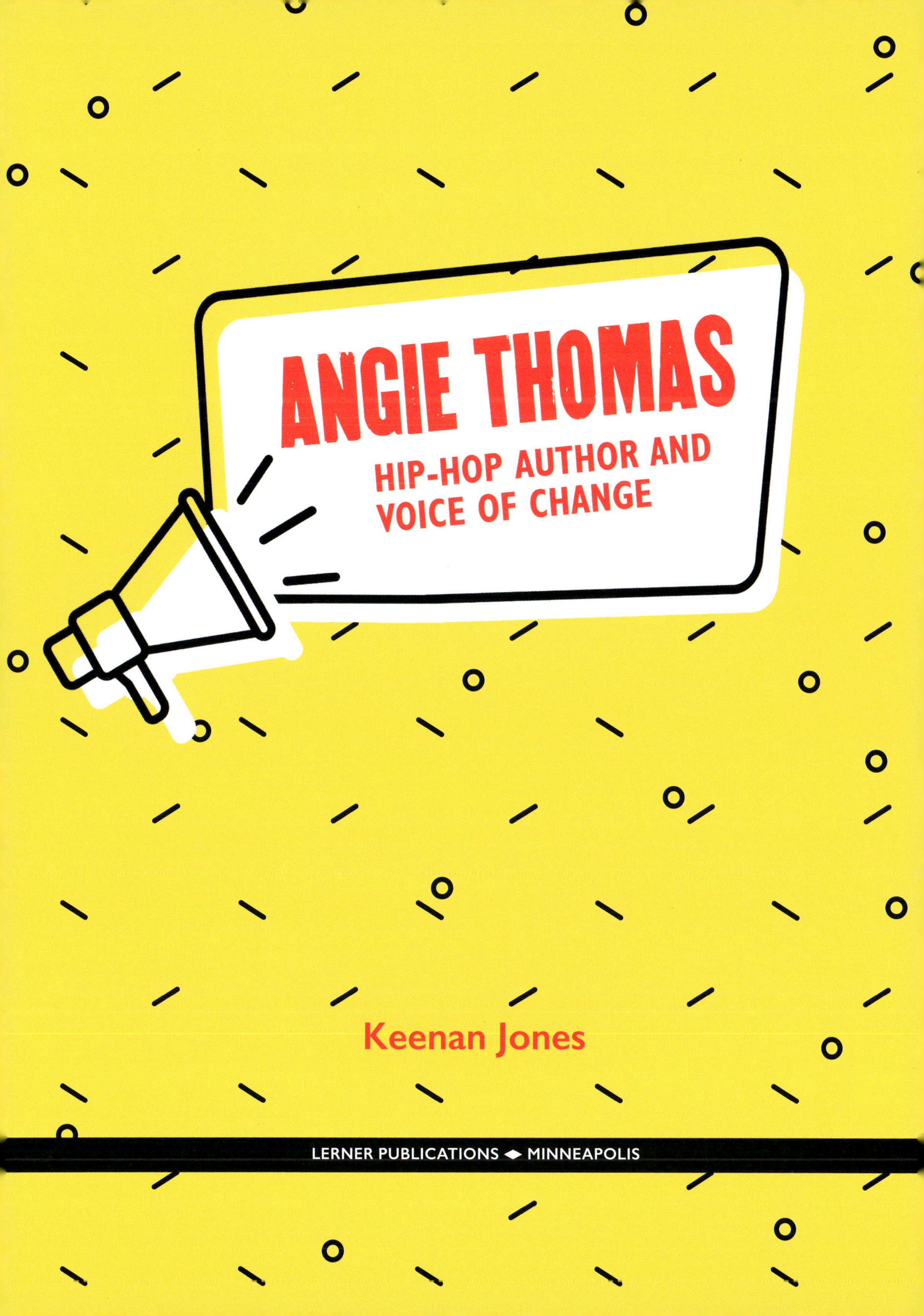

ANGIE THOMAS

HIP-HOP AUTHOR AND VOICE OF CHANGE

Keenan Jones

LERNER PUBLICATIONS ◆ MINNEAPOLIS

This book is dedicated to Black authors and visionaries, both past and present, who laid the foundation for us to be free and to speak our truths in America.

Lerner Publications Company
An imprint of Lerner Publishing Group, Inc.
241 First Avenue North
Minneapolis, MN 55401 USA

For reading levels and more information, look up this title at www.lernerbooks.com.

Main body text set in Rotis Serif Std 55 Regular. Typeface provided by Adobe Systems.

Editor: Ashley Kuehl

Library of Congress Cataloging-in-Publication Data

Names: Jones, Keenan, author.
Title: Angie Thomas : hip-hop author and voice of change / Keenan Jones.
Description: Minneapolis : Lerner Publications, 2025. | Series: Gateway biographies | Includes bibliographical references and index. | Audience: Ages 9–14 | Audience: Grades 4–6 | Summary: "Angie Thomas was a teen rapper before attaining a degree in creative writing. Her novels The Hate U Give and On the Come Up are both New York Times bestsellers. Discover her life and career"– Provided by publisher.
Identifiers: LCCN 2024022808 (print) | LCCN 2024022809 (ebook) | ISBN 9798765649145 (library binding) | ISBN 9798765661772 (paperback) | ISBN 9798765654750 (epub)
Subjects: LCSH: Thomas, Angie—Juvenile literature. | Authors, American—21st century—Biography—Juvenile literature. | African American women—Biography—Juvenile literature. | LCGFT: Biographies.
Classification: LCC PS3620.H624626 Z69 2025 (print) | LCC PS3620.H624626 (ebook) | DDC 813/.6 [B]—dc23/eng/20240530

LC record available at https://lccn.loc.gov/2024022808
LC ebook record available at https://lccn.loc.gov/2024022809

Manufactured in the United States of America
1-1011060-53494-8/5/2024

TABLE OF CONTENTS

Angie Thomas signs a copy of *The Hate U Give* in 2018.

On February 26, 2012, in Sanford, Florida, seventeen-year-old Trayvon Martin was walking to a store to buy candy. Along the way, George Zimmerman, a neighborhood watch volunteer, saw Trayvon. Then Zimmerman made a fast but permanent decision. Zimmerman decided that Trayvon was a threat and fatally shot the young man.

People across the country were outraged. To them, Trayvon represented millions of young Black boys who make daily trips to the store. As shocking and sad as Trayvon's death was, this event was not unique. It was part of a larger pattern of Black boys and men being killed. As the news about Trayvon spread, it sparked a movement. A new generation started to push back against society's historically poor treatment of Black people. These tragic events would inspire organizations as well as the next generation of artists, including writer Angie Thomas.

In early 2012, Thomas was a college graduate and aspiring writer who worked at a church. When she saw the news about Trayvon, she felt angry and sad but also motivated. She felt inspired to tell her story, the Black story, and to spark conversations. Thomas's debut novel, *The Hate U Give*, tells the story of a girl named Starr. She lives in inner-city America and sees her childhood friend gunned down by police. The book was a plea for love, respect, and empathy toward the Black community. Little did its author know that her words would not only spark a movement but would ultimately help change the course of how we talk about race in the United States.

Demonstrators call for justice in Stanford, Florida, after the shooting of Trayvon Martin.

A woman signs her name to a memorial for Trayvon Martin in Miami, Florida, on the tenth anniversary of his death.

Growing Up in Jackson, Mississippi

Angie Thomas was born on September 20, 1988, in Jackson, Mississippi. The city has a long history of racial segregation, or people being separated by race. Before the Civil Rights Movement of the 1950s and 1960s, Black people and white people had separate churches, schools, parks, playgrounds, restaurants, and bathrooms. The nationwide movement focused on ending segregation in the United States. It was one of the biggest movements in American history. Jackson was a key city in the fight for equality. Its public library was famous for its sit-ins and protests.

MEDGAR EVERS

Medgar Evers was an activist in Mississippi in the 1950s and 1960s. He organized voter registration drives, events to help Black people register to vote. He also started boycotts of companies that wouldn't serve Black people. During a boycott, many people agree to not buy from or support a business. A white man fatally shot Evers in 1963, when Evers was thirty-seven. Angie Thomas's mother, who was a child at the time, heard the gunshots from her home in the neighborhood.

Angie grew up in the same neighborhood as civil rights icon Medgar Evers, who had stood up for Black rights in Jackson during the 1960s. Although the city is rich in civil rights history, it has present-day problems. Angie grew up amid poverty and gun violence. She says, "When I was six, I was at the park, and two drug dealers decided to recreate the wild west with a shootout. . . . I ended up running out of the crossfire." Angie's mother wanted her to experience life beyond the troubles in their neighborhood. Angie said, "The very next day, Mom took me to the library, because she wanted me to see that there was more to the world than what I saw that day."

Hip-hop music was a big influence during Angie's teen years. She began writing rhymes and even appeared in *Right On!*, a teen magazine devoted to Black celebrities.

Hip-hop gave Angie an outlet to express herself, but it was also one of the only ways she thought she could be successful. She later said, "When I didn't see myself in books, I saw myself in hip-hop. . . . Rappers would tell me stories about kids like me." One of her influences was the late rapper Tupac Shakur. In addition to being a multiplatinum artist (an artist whose albums sold at least two million copies), he was an actor and an activist. His parents were members of the Black Panther Party. In the 1960s, this activist organization focused on Black power

HIP-HOP HISTORY

Black artists in the Bronx, New York, created the genre of hip-hop in the early 1970s. The music was a way to bring people together in the wake of the poverty, violence, and drugs that were affecting inner-city communities. It has grown into a global genre of music, made and enjoyed by people from cultures around the world. Hip-hop has been a beacon of light in the Black community, uplifting many people in their toughest times.

and armed self-defense to fight against police brutality. He died at the age of twenty-five. Despite his short career, he left a legacy in hip-hop, and his records continued to sell after his death.

Another big influence on young Angie was the late multiplatinum singer Left Eye, from the group TLC. One

TUPAC SHAKUR

Tupac Shakur was inducted into the Rock & Roll Hall of Fame in 2017, twenty years after his death. A Hall of Fame essay about Tupac described him as "a lightning rod, a screen on which millions of people projected their feelings about rap, race, and young Black men in America." His rap career lasted only five years, but he remains one of the most popular artists in history with over seventy-five million records sold worldwide.

TLC members Tionne "T-Boz" Watkins, Lisa "Left Eye" Lopes, and Rozonda "Chilli" Thomas pose for a photo.

of TLC's major hits in 1994 was the song "Waterfalls." The song encourages people not to chase waterfalls, a metaphor for dangerous or risky behavior. It reminds them that life is valuable. This song empowered many people during tough times, including Angie. Kids at school had been bullying her, and she was having suicidal thoughts.

Angie's mom grew concerned for her mental health but noticed that her daughter loved TLC. Her mom managed to track down the number to the group's studio to try to connect with Left Eye. One day, while Angie was watching TV, her mother interrupted her with a phone call. Angie's hero, Left Eye, was on the line. She gave Angie some powerful words, saying, "I've never met you, but I've got a feeling you can do something great one day, and you can't do it if you take your life." Those words had a big impact on teenage Angie, inspiring her to have hope.

After high school, Angie went on to attend Belhaven, a mostly white private Christian school in Jackson. Her college was in a part of town that was extremely different from the majority Black neighborhood where she had grown up. During these years, Angie began to really see the differences between Black and white culture at her school. Her white classmates didn't see the guns and poverty she had experienced growing up. It was as if they lived in two different worlds in the same city.

Belhaven is a Christian college in Jackson, Mississippi.

A man prays in front of a mural of Oscar Grant at the spot where he was slain.

In 2009, while Angie was attending Belhaven, police officers killed another young Black man. Oscar Grant had been hanging out with friends on New Year's Eve in Oakland, California. They decided to take the train home instead of driving. In the early hours of the morning, police officers responded to calls about a fight. When they arrived, they detained Oscar and his friends. After a brief struggle, one of the officers shot Oscar in the back. Witnesses recorded the shooting on their phones. The officer was charged with murder, but he pleaded not guilty and served only two years in prison.

Back in Jackson, Angie was angered to hear that police had killed another unarmed Black man. At her college, she found herself in conflict with her classmates, who couldn't understand why so many people were frustrated by the killing. Instead of staying angry, she picked up her pencil and began writing. Angie wrote a short story about a boy named Khalil and a girl named Starr. Partly, she hoped that it would help her classmates understand her perspective. But more important, she did it for herself.

In 2011 Angie was the first Black student to graduate from Belhaven's creative writing program.

Black Lives Matter Movement

George Zimmerman killed Trayvon Martin in February 2012. In July 2013, Zimmerman was found not guilty of murder. Many folks took to social media to talk about the country's long history of failure to value Black lives. But other people online defended and excused Zimmerman's actions. They blamed Trayvon, his family, and his actions for his death.

Alicia Garza lived in Oakland then. Her job was to organize for workers' rights. Garza was saddened and angered by the acquittal, or not-guilty verdict. She wrote a series of posts on Facebook titled, "A Love Letter to Black People." She ended one of her final posts with, "Our lives matter." Her close friend, Patrisse Cullors, responded

Black Lives Matter cofounders Ayọ Tometi, Alicia Garza, and Patrisse Cullors gather for an event in New York City in 2015.

to the posts by saying, "#BlackLivesMatter." The Black Lives Matter movement was born.

The hashtag spread slowly at first. But in 2014, white police officers killed two more unarmed Black men. After the deaths of Missouri's Michael Brown and New York's Eric Garner, the movement grew more quickly. Black Lives Matter focuses on three major problems. Police brutality is when police officers use excessive force against civilians. Racial profiling happens when a person is suspected of a crime based on the color of their skin. And racial inequality is when people of certain racial backgrounds have more or fewer opportunities available to them, only because of their race. These issues have affected Black people throughout US history, dating back to slavery.

A man carries a Black Lives Matter flag at a 2020 march in Texas.

Black Lives Matter aims to draw attention to this unfairness and fight for Black lives. More than thirty Black Lives Matter chapters have sprung up across the country, each unique to their local Black population. The movement has inspired other organizations, such as the Breathe Act, which encourages communities to redirect money from police budgets toward community services. Another is the Black Futures Lab, founded by Alicia Garza, which helps Black communities get more involved with politics and local laws.

Between 2014 and May 2020, #BlackLivesMatter was used on Twitter (now X) 39.2 million times. Then, in the spring of 2020, police officers in Minneapolis,

Minnesota, killed George Floyd, an unarmed Black man. Protests began in Minneapolis and spread around the world. After that, the hashtag was shared over 100 million times. At least sixty-two American companies posted about Black Lives Matter on their social media channels during the protests. Social media helped amplify the message.

Artwork honoring Floyd

GEORGE FLOYD

George Floyd's murder in Minneapolis in May 2020 sparked the largest racial justice protests in the United States since the Civil Rights Movement. Many Black activists saw Floyd's death as a symbol of injustice. Outside of the United States, the United Kingdom had the largest Black Lives Matter protest. New Zealand, France, and Colombia saw huge demonstrations too.

The Black Lives Matter movement has inspired a new generation of protests against police violence toward Black people. It highlights systemic racism—when the laws and practices in society give certain groups an unfair advantage because of their race. Followers feel inspired by the hope of living in a world where everybody has an equal chance at success.

The Hate U Give

Back in 2015, before Black Lives Matter spread so far and wide, Thomas was feeling angry about the deaths of more unarmed Black men. In August of the previous year, a white police officer in Ferguson, Missouri, had killed eighteen-year-old Michael Brown. The following month, in Cleveland, Ohio, a white officer had shot and killed twelve-year-old Tamir Rice. Both officers left their jobs but neither was charged for wrongdoing.

As protests continued across the country, Thomas poured her rage and frustrations back into her short story. While she was employed as a secretary at a church in Mississippi, she continued to write. Thomas says, "I wrote while I was working . . . yeah, all of those curse words were written in church." Angie was empowered to finish what she had started. Her short story grew into a novel.

The story's main character, Starr, is a sixteen-year-old Black girl growing up in the inner city. She attends a

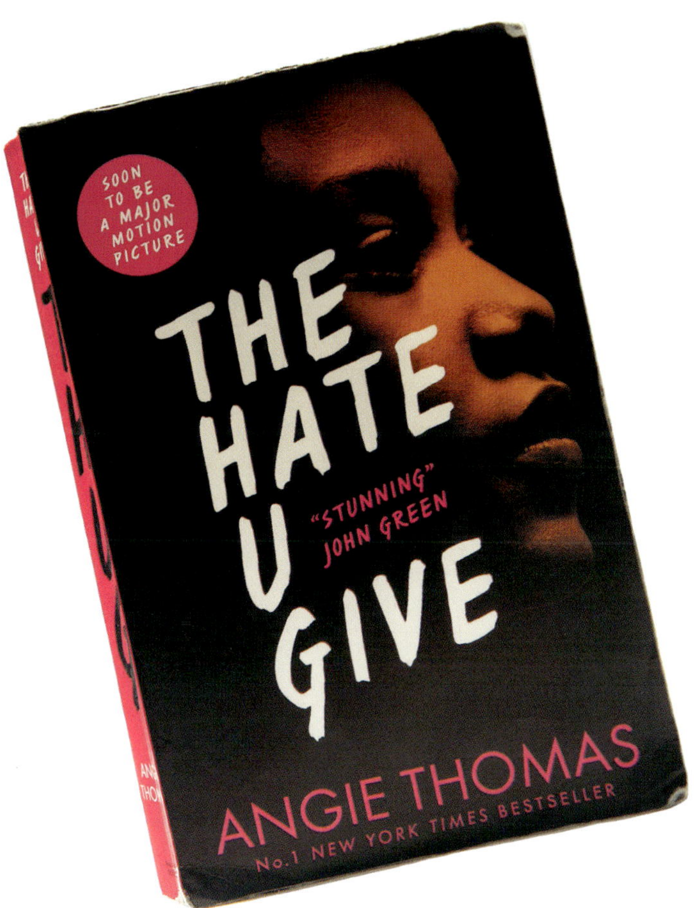

The Hate U Give **is a bestselling book that sparked conversations around police brutality.**

school in a wealthy suburb, navigating two very different worlds. The story takes a turn when Starr and her best friend, Khalil, are pulled over by police. A struggle happens with Khalil, and the police shoot him. Starr has a growing awareness that the lives of Black people are less important in the eyes of the police. Instead of receiving protection from police, Black people are more likely to be harmed.

Thomas presents *The Hate U Give* at the Massachusetts Conference for Women in Boston, Massachusetts, in 2019.

Thomas was determined that this book would make it into the world. She had been sending her other work to literary agents. A literary agent can help an author land a book deal by sending the work to publishers. By 2015 literary agents had already rejected her other children's book manuscript sixty times.

Thomas's hard work and perseverance finally paid off when she contacted We Need Diverse Books, a nonprofit created to promote diversity in children's books. Thomas submitted her work to one of their inaugural contests and won a cash prize. With the money from the award, she was able to get a new laptop, but more important, a panel of judges told her that her novel was good. The title of her book *The Hate U Give* comes from Tupac Shakur, whose group Thug Life had an album that shared the group's name. The Thug part of the name stood for "the hate u give."

On February 28, 2017, Balzer + Bray, part of publisher HarperCollins, finally published *The Hate U Give.* The book achieved immediate success, debuting at number one on the *New York Times* bestseller list. It also won the ALA's William C. Morris YA Debut Award, a Boston Globe–Horn Book Award, the UK Waterstones Children's Book Prize, and the German Youth Literature Award.

TUPAC'S "DEAR MAMA"

In 1995 Tupac Shakur released his hit song "Dear Mama," dedicated to his mother, Afeni Shakur. She had been a member of the Black Panther Party. Tupac was raised by his mother, and they endured some tough times when he was a child. Despite their hardships, he praised his mother as being a Black queen who did all she could to provide for them. The song went on to achieve triple platinum, one the highest honors for a song. Many rap critics call it one of the top ten songs of all time.

From Book to Movie

In 2018 *The Hate U Give* had been on the *New York Times* bestseller list for eighty-five weeks.

Like many great books of recent times, *The Hate U Give* was destined to become a film. It had been the subject of a bidding war in 2016, with Fox 2000 winning the rights. As filming began, Thomas was on set for an in-depth look into how scenes were shot. She gave input on the sets, from houses to the neighborhood to Starr's bedroom. She was even able to bring her mother to visit the set!

Thomas and actors Amandla Stenberg and Regina Hall (*front row*) and director George Tillman Jr. and actor Russel Hornsby (*back row*) at a 2018 event

The movie was released in October 2018. The movie strikes a balance between a coming-of-age story nestled in a family narrative and an emotional drama. The cast of characters shows truths about romance and receiving love from one's parents with a touch of grit that people relate to.

George Tillman Jr. and Amandla Stenberg at a 2018 screening of *The Hate U Give*

The film included a star-studded cast and crew. Black director George Tillman Jr. had helped direct and produce iconic films involving Black American culture, such as *Soul Food* and *Barbershop.* Starr was played by Amandla Stenberg, an up-and-coming actor who had played a key role in the *Hunger Games* movies. With a strong narrative rhythm and outstanding performances, Tillman was able to give voice to an urgent matter of social justice in the United States.

In an interview, Thomas talked about what the movie was able to bring to the story that the book wasn't and vice versa. She said, "I think that with the book, things may feel more intimate at times—after all, the reader is in the character's head. But with the film, the power of some scenes hit harder. . . . For instance, I can describe a protest, but it's another thing to see hundreds of people participating in one."

The Hate U Give was in theaters for fifteen weeks before moving to streaming platforms. The online movie review platform Rotten Tomatoes gave the film a 97 percent rating. Film reviewer David Reddish wrote, "*The Hate U Give* is not an easy pill to swallow by design: [they] want to start a conversation. They succeed in their intentions, creating one of the best films of the past decade, and a showcase for Stenberg."

On the Come Up

Thomas, a child of hip-hop, would soon write a book giving praise to the genre that had inspired her when she was younger. She said, "Hip-hop was the form of storytelling that resonated with me the most. . . . I didn't connect with many books because it was hard to find stories that reflected me. Rappers described my life and the lives around me." Thomas felt empowered by these storytellers. As she described it, "Hip-hop validated me. It also showed me that I had a voice and that it was worth using."

Hip-hop and break dancing are rich and long-standing forms of artistic expression in the Black community.

Since *The Hate U Give* was an instant classic, Thomas could feel the pressure to write a great follow-up. She had to make some decisions, such as not including any characters from *The Hate U Give*. She also took her own advice of writing this book for herself, not her fans.

Thomas wrote *On the Come Up* for her younger self, the young Angie who always wanted to be a rapper. The two books are connected through the same fictional neighborhood of Garden Heights but with new characters. Brianna in *On the Come Up* mirrored more of Thomas's personal upbringing. Thomas had never experienced what *The Hate U Give*'s Starr experienced. That book had been a response to her frustrations about police brutality.

On the Come Up was published on February 5, 2019. The story is told through the eyes of sixteen-year-old Brianna "Bri" Jackson. Her mother is a former drug addict who is behind on her rent. Bri is an MC, or performer of rap. She loves hip-hop, yet her schoolwork is slipping. Bri's ultimate goal is to be crowned the queen MC in hopes of getting enough money to care for her mother and brother. This story is Thomas's tribute to hip-hop culture, family, food, and pop culture. *On the Come Up* won the 2020 Youth Literature Award from the Mississippi Institute of Arts and Letters. It also debuted at number one on the *New York Times* bestseller list.

In March 2020, Thomas released *Find Your Voice: A Guided Journal for Writing Your Truth.* In this journal, Thomas offers writing tips, daily exercises, quotes, and graphic organizers. The following month, Belhaven University created the Angie Thomas Writers Scholarship. Students enrolled in Belhaven's creative writing program may apply for the scholarship, and one winner is chosen each year.

Thomas at the Spelman College screening of the *On the Come Up* film in 2022

The first award went to Imani Skipwith of Jackson, Mississippi, covering tuition, room, and board for four years. Thomas said, "It's an honor to know that such a brilliant young woman will benefit from a scholarship in my honor. . . . I have no doubt that Imani will soar under the guidance of the entire Belhaven family."

Just like *The Hate U Give*, *On the Come Up* soon became a film featuring a star-studded cast. Often when

Director Sanaa Lathan, Jamila C. Gray, and Da'Vine Joy Randolph (*left to right*) at a 2022 screening of *On the Come Up*

books become movies, authors don't get much say in the movie's look and feel. But in this case, the director, Sanaa Lathan, loved the book and gave Thomas an opportunity to be involved. *This Is Us* writer-director Kay Oyegun wrote the screenplay. The cast includes notables such as hip-hop legend Method Man and comedian and actor Mike Epps. The film debuted in September 2022.

Thomas at the *On the Come Up* premiere at the 2022 Toronto International Film Festival

Concrete Rose

The *New York Times* called Angie Thomas's third book, *Concrete Rose*, "a love song for Black lives." The book was published in January 2021. Thomas was beginning to cement herself as a force in publishing.

Concrete Rose includes a character from *The Hate U Give*, Maverick Carter. In this story, seventeen-year-old Maverick is the protagonist. The son of a gang leader, Maverick feels pressure to follow in his father's footsteps. He sells drugs to make money for his family, but his life turns upside down when he becomes a father. *Concrete*

Thomas speaks at the Mississippi Book Festival in Jackson, Mississippi, in 2022.

Rose explores the challenges that some Black males experience in America, including gangs, struggles with identity, systemic racism, and incarcerated family members. This story argues that it's never too late to turn your life around.

Soon after writing *Concrete Rose*, Thomas collaborated with five other nationally acclaimed Black young adult authors. Writer Dhonielle Clayton had been inspired by her niece, who wondered why Black girls are rarely featured in love stories. This was soon after the 2020 COVID-19 pandemic began, and many people were feeling scared and sad. Clayton connected with her favorite Black female young adult authors, who decided to put their talents together and create a collection of stories about Black teens in love.

Blackout, released in 2021, was written by Dhonielle Clayton, Tiffany D. Jackson, Nic Stone, Angie Thomas, Ashley Woodfolk, and Nicola Yoon. The book showed the power of Black art in a time of uncertainty. It was another example of Thomas's commitment to creating work that empowers others.

Diversity in Publishing

Thomas had witnessed the importance of books about Black kids with her debut novel. She, along with many teachers and researchers, believe that reading Black stories and perspectives is a critical step to confronting systemic racism. Thomas believes that literature can empower the next generation of leaders and that the key to equipping young people for the future lies in diverse storytelling. Through her own fictional characters, Thomas works to create mirrors and windows so that people can see themselves or see people unlike themselves. That helps people build empathy for one another.

Readers of Thomas's books might understand what it means for a Black person who attends an all-white school to code-switch. That's when a Black person adjusts how they walk or talk to fit in with the dominant white culture. When Thomas writes, her priority is Black kids. That's because they don't have enough books about themselves. She has even called on her own publisher, HarperCollins, to advocate for more diversity in publishing. Diversity must be not only in books but in the people who make them.

In December 2020, the *New York Times* published, "How White Is the Book Industry?" It looks into how the publishing industry can improve on making books for people of color. The newspaper had studied how many authors of color published books between 1950 and 2018. Of the 7,124 books for which they could identify the author's race, 95 percent were written by white people. Those numbers are similar to the statistics of those who acquire and edit books, which was 85 percent white.

But things are slowly changing. Lee & Low Books, one of the nation's leading Black-owned publishing companies, also did a survey in 2023. They found that 72.5 percent

It's important for people of all backgrounds to see themselves reflected in books.

of the publishing industry overall was white, compared with 5.3 identifying as Black, African American, or Afro Caribbean. In 2024 the Cooperative Children's Book Center said that of the 3,491 books they received, 40 percent had been created by a person of color.

Thomas believes that Black stories and perspectives are one step in confronting systemic racism in America. She says, "I believe in the power of books and how they shape young people for the future. . . . I'm very hopeful that we're giving them better tools so that they could be better leaders than any of us ever imagined." She has been able to get the ear of young audiences through the power of diverse storytelling, creating mirrors and windows for young people of all backgrounds.

But as Thomas continues to advocate for diverse titles, she has encountered book bans. Public and school libraries have taken *The Hate U Give* off the shelves, even in her home state of Mississippi. Book banning is the

Thomas and George M. Johnson speak at the Defending the Right to Read panel at the LA Times Festival of Books in 2023.

Marchers in Coral Gables, Florida, protest book bans in 2023.

removal of a book from shelves because people may not agree with what has been written. People, often parents, who ban or challenge books argue that reading the books could harm young people. One challenge against *The Hate U Give* said that it contained violence that young people should not read about.

Thomas's books, along with many others across the nation that deal with race, have been banned in an

Activists hand out banned books and T-shirts in 2023 to speak out for people's freedom to read in South Miami, Florida.

attempt to keep them from minors. Thomas spoke at Mississippi's first Banned Book Festival in 2024, calling the act of banning her book disappointing. Thomas believes that people should have the right to read what they want to read. A group called Pen America tracks book challenges and bans in the United States. Their research has shown that most books that are banned involve race or characters and themes from marginalized groups. Marginalized groups include people who are discriminated against because of their race, gender identity, abilities, language, and other factors.

Authors, librarians, teachers, and others are fighting back against book bans, but bans and challenges continue to grow. This fight for (and against) diverse books has become a battleground in politics, schools, and communities across the country. It is rooted in the systemic racism that continues to exist in the United States.

Continued Success

In 2023 Angie released her first middle grade novel, the first in a series, to give Black girls a space in fantasy. Inspired by the Black folktale "The People Could Fly," the series Nic Blake and the Remarkables is about a Black girl who has exceptional powers. The protagonist was a side character in another novel Thomas wrote, which was rejected. In the first book, Nic Blake discovers a secret about her father and embarks on a dangerous journey to save him. Thomas had dreamed of writing this book for more than fifteen years.

The Angie Thomas Writers Scholarship continues to support students in the creative writing program at Belhaven University. Thomas amplifies the scholarship by encouraging students to apply. In early 2024, Maya McFadden was the fifth person to win this award. Maya's writing included folklore, history, and myth. The scholarship will allow her to focus on her studies while improving her craft. Thomas and Belhaven have stayed

Thomas remains engaged in initiatives to promote inclusion and diversity in literature.

committed to their mission of uplifting underrepresented voices in literature.

Thomas continues to engage in public speaking events across the country, such as a 2024 keynote speech at a Massachusetts private school's thirty-fifth Martin Luther King Jr. Day celebration. Her speech included the acronym HOPE, which means: Have Optimism, Perspective, and Endurance. Thomas also hosts writing groups to support up-and-coming writers, demonstrating her commitment to helping writers find their voice.

Many people have pointed to the positive changes Thomas's books have made for young Black readers. But humble by nature, Thomas argues that others paved the way for her career. She referred to Walter Dean Myers (1937–2014), a prolific Black children's book writer whose life's mission was to put those missing diverse voices on bookshelves. In 1986 Myers published an essay in the *New York Times*, arguing for more books for and about Black kids.

Thomas believes publishing would not have changed if not for such voices. She says, "It took someone like Walter Dean Myers, calling out publishing in a piece for the *New York Times* and saying that we don't see enough diverse books." Thomas believes she benefited from people such as Myers, saying, "So if people say 'oh, *The Hate U Give* changed publishing,' well no. I reaped benefits from the work that had already been done by the people before me."

From touring at schools around the country to giving keynotes and hosting workshops on writing, Thomas is leaving her physical and digital footprint as a writer, author, and speaker. Having achieved much success by selling millions of books in such a short time, she continues to remain humble and focused on uplifting voices around the world. Thomas's voice is unique to this generation. Her work is likely to stand the test of time.

IMPORTANT DATES

1988 Angie Thomas is born in Jackson, Mississippi.

2009 Police in Oakland kill Oscar Grant.

2011 Thomas graduates from Belhaven University.

2012 George Zimmerman kills Trayvon Martin in Sanford, Florida.

2015 Thomas receives the first ever Walter Dean Myers Grant.

2017 HarperCollins publishes *The Hate U Give*. It becomes a *New York Times* bestseller.

2018 Fox 2000 Pictures releases the feature film version of *The Hate U Give*.

2019 *On the Come Up* is published and becomes a *New York Times* bestseller.

2020 Thomas wins Mississippi's Youth Literature Award.

Thomas publishes the *Find Your Voice* journal.

The inaugural Angie Thomas Writers Scholarship is awarded.

2021 *Concrete Rose* is published.

Blackout, a novel Thomas coauthored with five other Black writers, is released.

2022 The feature film version of *On the Come Up* is released.

2023 The first novel in Nic Blake and the Remarkables, Thomas's fantasy novel series, is published.

2024 The fifth annual Angie Thomas Writers Scholarship is awarded to Maya McFadden.

SOURCE NOTES

10–11 Lucy Feldman, "How TLC's Left Eye Helped Save *The Hate U Give* Author Angie Thomas' Life," *Time*, February 5, 2019, https://time.com/5521258/angie-thomas-on-the-come-up-book/.

11 Feldman.

12 Allan Light, "Hall of Fame Essay," Rock & Roll Hall of Fame, accessed May 19, 2024, https://rockhall.com/inductees/tupac-shakur/.

13–14 Feldman, "How TLC's Left Eye Helped Save *The Hate U Give* Author Angie Thomas' Life."

16 Isabella Mercado, "The Black Lives Matter Movement: An Origin Story," Underground Railroad Education Center, accessed May 18, 2024, https://undergroundrailroadhistory.org/the-black-lives-matter-movement-an-origin-story/.

20 Afua Hirsch, "Angie Thomas: The Debut Novelist Who Turned Racism and Police Violence into a Bestseller," *Guardian* (US edition), March 26, 2017, https://www.theguardian.com/books/2017/mar/26/angie-thomas-the-debut-novelist-who-turned-racism-and-police-violence-into-a-bestseller.

26 "Exclusive Q&A with The Hate U Give Author Angie Thomas." *Books-a-million* (blog), accessed May 14, 2024, https://blog.booksamillion.com/posts/exclusive-q-a-with-the-hate-u-give-author-angie-thomas.

26 David Reddish, "We Need to Talk about Amandla Stenberg, One of Her Generation's Brightest Queer Talents," Queerty, September 25, 2021, https://www.queerty.com/need-talk-amandla-stenberg-one-generations-brightest-queer-talents-20210925.

26 Teen Vogue staff, "Angie Thomas Talks 'on the Come up' and Hip-Hop Influence: Cover Reveal," *Teen Vogue*, August 28, 2020, https://www.teenvogue.com/story/angie-thomas-on-the-come-up-paperback-cover-reveal.

29 Associated Press, "Teen Receives Scholarship Honoring 'The Hate U Give' Author," Spectrum News 1, April 29, 2020, https://spectrumlocalnews.com/nc/coastal/ap-top-news/2020/04/29/teen-receives-scholarship-honoring-the-hate-u-give-author.

32 "Angie Thomas's 'Concrete Rose' Is a Love Song for Young Black Lives," *New York Times Book Review*, February 18, 2021, https://www.nytimes.com/2021/02/18/books/review/concrete-rose-angie-thomas.html.

35–36 Paulina Cachero, "Author Angie Thomas on How Books Are Transforming the Next Generation: 'They're Realizing Their Power,'" *Time*, August 6, 2020, https://time.com/5875827/author-angie-thomas-time-100-talks/.

41 "Interview: Angie Thomas on Her New Fantasy Series, Nic Blake and the Remarkables," OWLconnected, March 30, 2023, https://owlconnected.com/archives/interview-angie-thomas.

SELECTED BIBLIOGRAPHY

"Author Angie Thomas Writes to 'Mirror' Young, Black Readers." NPR, February 5, 2019. https://www.npr.org/2019/01/31/690391879/author-angie-thomas-writes-to-mirror-young-black-readers.

"The Black Panther Party." National Archives. Accessed May 17, 2024. https:/www.archives.gov/research/african-americans/black-power/black-panthers#:~:text=The%20Black%20Panther%20Party%20for,defense%2C%20particularly%20against%20police%20brutality.

"The Civil Rights Movement: U.S. History Primary Source Timeline. Library of Congress." Library of Congress. Accessed May 17, 2024. https://www.loc.gov/classroom-materials/united-states-history-primary-source-timeline/post-war-united-states-1945-1968/civil-rights-movement/.

Dickinson, Kari. "CCBC's Latest Diversity Statistics Show Increasing Number of Diverse Books for Children and Teens." University of Wisconsin–Madison, School of Education, June 13, 2023. https://education.wisc.edu/news/ccbcs-latest-diversity-statistics-show-increasing-number-of-diverse-books-for-children-and-teens/.

Hirsch, Afua. "Angie Thomas: The Debut Novelist Who Turned Racism and Police Violence into a Bestseller." *Guardian* (US edition), March 26, 2017. https://www.theguardian.com/books/2017/mar/26/angie-thomas-the-debut-novelist-who-turned-racism-and-police-violence-into-a-bestseller.

Jones, Iyana. "Angie Thomas Ventures into Middle Grade." *Publishers Weekly*, August 31, 2022. https://www.publishersweekly.com/pw/by-topic/childrens/childrens-authors/article/90215-pw-talks-with-angie-thomas.html.

Mitchell, Jerry, and Ann Marie Cunningham. "Mississippi's Own Angie Thomas: Her Most Popular Book Is Missing from Library Shelves." Mississippi Today, March 16, 2023. https://mississippitoday.org/2023/03/16/angie-thomas-mississippi-book-ban/.

Schaub, Michael. "Angie Thomas Sponsors New Writing Scholarship." *Kirkus Reviews*, February 14, 2020. https:/www.kirkusreviews.com/news-and-features/articles/angie-thomas-sponsors-new-writing-scholarship/?__hstc=232449024.94ddc56625e156b8cc939cfcb6ddfbfc.1711584000188.1711584000189.1711584000190.1&__hssc=232449024.1.1711584000191&__hsfp=892594048.

Tesema, Martha. "Angie Thomas's 'Concrete Rose' Is a Love Song for Young Black Lives." *New York Times*, February 18, 2021. https://www.nytimes.com/2021/02/18/books/review/concrete-rose-angie-thomas.html.

LEARN MORE

Britannica Kids: Black Lives Matter
https://kids.britannica.com/kids/article/Black-Lives-Matter/632612

Chang, Jeff. *Can't Stop, Won't Stop: A Hip-Hop History*. With Dave "Davey D" Cook. New York: Wednesday Books, 2021.

Jackson, Tom. *Kendrick Lamar and Tupac Shakur: Influential Rappers*. Minneapolis: Lerner Publications, 2025.

Kiddle: Hip-Hop Facts for Kids
https://kids.kiddle.co/Hip_hop

PBS Learning Media: Civil Rights
https://tpt.pbslearningmedia.org/collection/civil/

Smith, Sherri L. *What Is the Civil Rights Movement?* New York: Penguin Workshop, 2020.

INDEX

PHOTO ACKNOWLEDGMENTS

Images: Paras Griffin/Getty Images, p.2; AP Photo/Rogelio V. Solis, pp.4, 32, 40; Gary W. Green/Orlando Sentinel/Tribune News Service/Getty Images, p. 8; AP Photo/Lynne Sladky, p. 9; Distributed by AP, courtesy of Wikimedia Commons (PD), p. 10; Al Pereira/Michael Ochs Archives/Getty Images, p. 12; Jeff Kravitz/FilmMagic/Getty Images, p. 13; Chad Robertson Media/Shutterstock, p. 14; The Blinking Eye/Stockimo/Alamy, p. 15; Slaven Vlasic/Getty Images, p. 17; AP Photo/Stuart Villanueva /The Galveston County Daily News, p. 18; Alexi Rosenfeld/Getty Images, p. 19; flab/Alamy, p. 21; Marla Aufmuth/Getty Images, p. 22; Ryan Theriot/Getty Images, p. 24; Eric Charbonneau/Getty Images, p. 25; fatihhoca/Getty Images, p. 27; Paras Griffin/Getty Images, p. 29; AP Photo/PICJER/imageSPACE/Sipa USA(Sipa, p. 31; Jerod Harris/Variety/Getty Images, p. 30; Gregg Vignal/Alamy, p. 35; Jason Armond/Los Angeles Times/Getty Images, p. 36; Carl Juste/Miami Herald/Tribune News Service/Getty Images, pp. 37, 38. Design element: Illerlok_xolms/Shutterstock.

Cover: Amanda Edwards/Getty Images; Illerlok_xolms/Shutterstock.